May 7th 2024

The Day the Earth Turned

Published 7th February 2024

Chapter 1: The Prelude to May 7, 2024

The Global Political Landscape : 2 elections for a war

As the dawn of 2024 approached, the world found itself at a precarious juncture. The echoes of past conflicts mingled with the rumblings of a future crisis, setting the stage for a year that could potentially reshape the contours of global power dynamics. At the heart of this looming storm was the intricate dance of geopolitics, where nations large and small played their parts in a game whose stakes could not be higher.

The previous years had seen a gradual but unmistakable shift in the geopolitical landscape. The resurgence of nationalism against the **NWO**, the retreat from globalization, and the intensification of rivalries had fragmented the post-Cold War order. Amidst this flux, two nations, the United States and Russia, continued their age-old ballet of competition and cooperation, each maneuvering for strategic advantage in a world that seemed increasingly multipolar now: **BRICS** against the US $.

The Election in March in Russia and 5th November in the US will be the catalyst for the war, one will remove the current president, and the other will set up a war to keep the incumbent.

Historical Tensions and the NATO-Russia Relationship

The relationship between **NATO** and **Russia** had long been characterized by a cycle of tension and temporary thaws, a reflection of the enduring legacy of the Cold War. The expansion of NATO eastward, since 1991, had been a thorn in the side of Russia, which viewed the alliance's approach to its borders as a direct threat to its security and sphere of influence. Confidence is broken. What did US will think if Russia will be in the Mexico border ? A total panic… **This historical backdrop set the stage for the events leading up to May 7, 2024, a day that would mark a significant escalation in these tensions: A WAVE.**

In the lead-up to this critical juncture, NATO's strategic posture had become increasingly aggressive. Huge Military exercises in Eastern Europe and the Baltics, intended as a show of strength and unity, were perceived by Russia as provocative acts. The alliance's commitment to defending its members was clear, but the strategy risked cornering a nation that prided itself on its military prowess and strategic depth.

The Role of Economic Confidence Model (ECM) in Predicting Conflict and Cycles

In this charged atmosphere, the *Economic Confidence Model* (ECM), a sophisticated forecasting tool developed in 70's by *Martin Armstrong* , emerged as a harbinger of turmoil. The ECM's algorithms or first AI, in fact, we must said, which analyzed vast amounts of economic data to predict periods of heightened conflict risk, had identified **Tuesday May 7, 2024 (and 8th)**, as **a peak** of geopolitical tension, it's THE day for the Russian new president to arise. This prediction lent a scientific veneer to the growing sense of unease among analysts and policymakers. The Wave 935 is interesting , and particularly *7th and 8th May 2024.*

The significance of the **ECM**'s forecast could not be overstated. It suggested that the confluence of economic pressures, military posturing, parking money and diplomatic stalemates was leading the world to a tipping point. The potential for conflict was further amplified by the planned swearing-in of the next president of Russia on May 7, an event that symbolized both continuity and change in Russian politics.

As the year 2024 unfolded, the world watched with bated breath. The actions of nations on the global stage, guided by a mix of strategic calculations, historical grievances, and the pursuit of national interests, were converging towards a moment that could either cement the existing order or shatter it entirely. The prelude to May 7 was not just a story of political maneuvering; it was a narrative of a world at the crossroads, grappling with the shadows of its past and the uncertainty of its future, the least we can say.

In this climate of heightened tension and anticipation, the stage was set for a series of events that could redefine the meaning of global security and the very concept of international law, already broken. The path to May 7, 2024, was paved with the complexities of modern geopolitics, where every action had repercussions, and every decision was a potential catalyst for conflict , not peace at all. War is coming and is near you not at the theater, civil and international war.

Chapter 2: The Catalysts of Conflict

The Election in March in Russia / in November in the US

The presidential election in Russia, held from *March 15 to March 17, 2024*, was more than just a political event; it was a barometer for the mood of the Russian populace and a reflection of the country's stance on the international stage. Despite the array of candidates, the election was less about who would win and more about the direction Russia would take in the ensuing critical months, **to survive as a nation.**

Nikolay Kharitonov of the *Independent Communist Alliance*, with his left-wing nationalist and communist inclinations, represented a segment of the population yearning for a return to Russia's past glories. ***Leonid Slutsky***'s *LDPR Party,* known for its ultranationalist and right-wing populist rhetoric, appealed to those who favored a more aggressive stance against the West. Meanwhile, ***Vladislav Davankov*** of the *New People Alliance SPPS Party* offered a more center-right, but still pro-Putin, perspective, suggesting a continuity of the current administration's policies.

However, the real intrigue lay not in the candidates themselves but in what their platforms revealed about Russia's internal dynamics and external ambitions. The election was a litmus test for **President Putin**'s enduring influence and the country's appetite for a more confrontational foreign policy.

The Swearing-In and Its Global Ramifications

The swearing-in of the Russian president on *May 7* was symbolic, not only marking the commencement of a new term but also coinciding with the peak of geopolitical tension identified by the **ECM**. This event is or was a focal point, a moment that could either solidify Russia's path towards aggressive posturing - the neocons exist also in Russia and open the door to a more hard approach.

The significance of this timing could not be understated. It was not merely coincidental but indicative of a deliberate alignment of domestic political milestones with broader strategic objectives. The new president's first actions and statements would be scrutinized for hints of Russia's future direction, particularly regarding its relations with **NATO** and the broader international community. Putin will be here or he will be replaced ? If replaced, a hardliner will set up Medvedev ?

The British-American Strategy : push, push, push

The British and American strategy to push NATO into a more confrontational stance with Russia was a high-stakes gamble. The proposal to send an expeditionary force to Ukraine and to impose a no-fly zone over Kyiv's territory was fraught with risks. Such moves were designed **to provoke a response,** to justify further escalation, and possibly, **to trigger a direct confrontation, with Russia. The British are proposing this takes place this May, coinciding with the swearing-in of the Russian president.**

Moreover, the justification for these actions was tied to the desire to influence the 2024 US election. The architects of this strategy believed that a summer conflict would sway public opinion and electoral outcomes. This Machiavellian approach to foreign policy was a dangerous game, leveraging global security for domestic political gains and power.

« We can destroy Russia in 3 days. »

Putin's speech on *February 24, 2022*, (*see the book War for the entire speech*) laid bare the deep-seated grievances and perceptions of betrayal that colored Russia's view of the West. "*The endless expansion of NATO, the abandonment of the Minsk Agreement, are not just provocations; they are betrayals of the path of peaceful conflict settlement,*" he declared, framing the narrative of Russia as a besieged fortress standing up against Western encroachment.

In contrast, **Adam Kinzinger'**s hawkish stance, a US Illinois neocon : "*We can destroy Russia in three days,*" and **Margarita Simonyan**'s (from RT TV station) chilling retort, "***We are the only country in the world that can destroy the United States in one hour,***" exemplified the dangerous rhetoric that contributed to the escalating tensions. Welcome to 2024! Nobody in Washington or London has any interest in peace.

These statements, while serving as rallying cries for their respective audiences, also underscored the perilous nature of the rhetoric being employed. They were not just words; they were potential preludes to action, with each side seemingly goading the other into making the first irreversible move.

As the world edged closer to ***May 7, 2024,*** the convergence of political events, strategic gambits, and bellicose rhetoric painted a picture of a world teetering on the brink. The March election in Russia was not just about who would lead the country; it was a precursor to a series of decisions that would determine the fate of global world. The backdrop of geopolitical maneuvering, strategic calculations, and the looming threat of conflict set the stage for a chapter in history that would be remembered for generations to come.

Chapter 3: The Mechanisms of War : Create one and

To force the outcome

The Proposed British Expeditionary Force to Ukraine

In the escalating tensions of early 2024, Britain's proposal to dispatch **an expeditionary force to Ukraine** represented a significant escalation in the **NATO**-Russia standoff. This move, ostensibly aimed at bolstering Ukrainian defenses, was also a clear signal to Russia and the international community. It underscored the West's readiness to take more direct action in the conflict, pushing the boundaries of conventional deterrence strategies.

The strategic implications of deploying British forces on Ukrainian soil were profound. Such a deployment would not only serve as a physical manifestation of **NATO**'s support for Ukraine but also as a potential catalyst for direct military confrontation. The official presence of foreign troops within striking distance of its borders was something Russia had long warned against, viewing it as a red line that could not be crossed without severe consequences. They know what they were doing from Suez Canal to China.

The No-Fly Zone Over Kyiv: A Precursor to Direct Confrontation

Equally contentious was the suggestion to impose a no-fly zone over Kyiv's territory. Advocates within NATO circles argued that it would protect civilian lives and critical infrastructure from aerial attacks.

However, the enforcement of a no-fly zone by NATO would require patrolling and potentially engaging with Russian aircraft, an act that could easily spiral into a broader conflict. The final aim ?

The very suggestion of a no-fly zone was a testament to the desperation and strategic recklessness that had come to characterize attempts to deter Russian aggression. It was a measure that, if implemented, would leave little room for diplomatic backtracking, pushing the situation closer to the brink of war. The 3rd one.

Deployment of NATO Troops to Norway and Finland

In a parallel development, the proposal to send NATO troops to Norway and Finland to confront Russia on its borders underscored the alliance's commitment to encircle Russia with a military presence. Moreover, Sweden joining NATO, beginning of 2024 was an other red alert for Russia, when Turkey gave its final approval. This move was designed not only as a deterrent but also as a preparatory step for a broader military engagement. The deployment in Scandinavia was a clear message of solidarity among NATO members and a demonstration of the alliance's willingness to defend its northern flank. Russia MUST be an enemy, or NATO has no purpose.

For Russia, the military buildup on its western and northern borders was an existential threat that could not be ignored. The Kremlin's response was measured yet firm, warning of reciprocal actions that would match or exceed NATO's provocations. The stage was set for a confrontation that could rapidly escalate beyond the confines of localized skirmishes. Welcome to May and July 2024 !

Chapter 4 - The Ukrainian Chessboard:

A Deliberate Provocation

The situation in Ukraine, deliberately set in motion to deplete Russian military forces, exemplified the complex web of strategies employed by NATO to weaken Russia.

The confluence of these strategic moves—**<u>Britain's proposal to send forces to Ukraine, the no-fly zone over Kyiv, and the deployment of NATO troops to Norway and Finland</u>**—outlined a complex matrix of military posturing and political signaling. Each action, while defensive in nature, carried the implicit threat of escalation, pushing the region, - and the world, closer to the brink of armed conflict.

These maneuvers reflected a broader strategy to deter Russian aggression through a show of force and solidarity among **NATO** members. However, they also risked provoking a response from Russia, which could interpret these moves as existential threats requiring a STRONG military answer with dedicated nukes. The potential for miscalculation is high, with each side viewing the other's actions through a lens of suspicion and hostility.

As the narrative of potential conflict unfolded, the mechanisms of war were set into motion, propelled by a mix of strategic imperatives and geopolitical ambitions. The decisions made in the lead-up to *May 7, 2024*, were not just about responding to immediate threats but about shaping the future security architecture of Europe and, by extension, the world. The interplay of military strategies, diplomatic initiatives, and political calculations created a tinderbox of tensions, where a single spark could ignite a conflagration that would be difficult to contain: the global fireworks.

Chapter 5: The Economic and Psychological Warfare

The Impact of Sanctions on the Ruble and Euro

As the geopolitical tensions escalated in the lead-up to *May 2024,* the economic front became a battleground of its own. Sanctions, a favored tool of European diplomatic pressure, began to weave their intricate tapestry of impact across the global economy like a boomerang inflation and stagflation everywhere. The Russian Ruble, already accustomed to the fluctuations wrought by international sanctions, faced a potential new onslaught. However, the unexpected casualty this time was the Euro, which began to experience a precipitous decline beginning in May 2024: the fall of EU and Euro: it's the fate of Euro: Going down, down, down. Things will become interesting in April with high volatility.

The 17'000 sanctions (and counting…) imposed on Russia were designed to be crippling, targeting key sectors of its economy, including **energy** exports, which are the lifeblood of the Russian economy. **Energy is Everything**, The intended effect was to isolate Russia economically, weaken its financial stability, and compel a change in its policies. However, the interconnectedness of the global economy meant that these sanctions also reverberated through the markets of the sanctioning countries: the boomerang effect , the French Minister of Economy said in 2022 : « *We will put Russian economy on his knees* », with GDP of +5% at the end of 2023 , it's the Europe on his knees, with debts and a banking sector that will implode in 2024. The fall of Swiss bank Credit Suisse was nothing last year, just an apero . On the other hand, Europe, heavily dependent on Russian energy and beyond , Europe found itself facing rising energy prices and a consequent economic slowdown, leading to the crash of the Euro (May-July 2024), and its banks (May to September 2024), as the debt with higher interest rates is killing each bank one after the other. Watch UBS, DB , they will land at 0 very soon, believe or not …

The collapse of European Banks is very probable from 7th May 2024. When China will sell EU and US debt, the knife will fall. Switzerland will feel it hardly, the last Swiss bank will be gone.

This economic downturn is further exacerbated by investor uncertainty and a loss of confidence in the Eurozone's economic stability. As the Euro began its decline, (since a long time) the European Central Bank found itself in a precarious position, needing to stabilize the currency while also navigating the economic fallout from escalating energy prices and the potential for a wider conflict with no ressource. I repeat with NO ressource.

Propaganda, Public Opinion, and the Demonization of Opponents

Parallel to the economic confrontation was the psychological warfare waged through media and propaganda. Both sides employed narratives designed to demonize the other, solidify internal support, and sway international opinion. The battle for hearts and minds was fought with every available tool—state-controlled media, social media platforms, and unofficial propaganda channels. Europe canceled in Feb 2022 all Russians channels from *RT to Sputnik*. A new kind of democracy was born.

In Russia, the portrayal of the West as aggressive, encroaching on Russian sovereignty, and disrespecting international norms became a common theme. In a sense, they are true where is international law? Seizing $300 billion of Russian Reserves and now saying they will hand them to Ukraine in this all-out war to destroy Russia, it is a strong warning to the rest of the world that NOBODY should have ANY reserves in ANY Western currency that can be seized.

Conversely, Western media focused on the narrative of Russian « aggression », the threat to European security, and the need for a unified response to uphold international law and protect « democratic values ». This narrative was bolstered by coverage of military movements, economic sanctions, and diplomatic efforts to isolate Russia.

The demonization of the opponent served a dual purpose: galvanizing domestic support and justifying the preparatory steps for potential conflict. France, Germany and Poland are ready to sacrifice their men for Ukraine… As public opinion was molded by these narratives, the psychological divide between the West and Russia deepened, creating an environment where dialogue and diplomacy became increasingly difficult. Switzerland is nowhere for peace talks. West is dying.

The War Equity Index and Financial Preparations for Conflict

The economic dimension of the unfolding crisis was underscored by the movements of the War Equity Index, a barometer for the financial market's expectations regarding conflict. As tensions escalated, the Index began to rise, last September 2023, before the 7th October event, reflecting investor anticipation of increased defense spending, the impact of sanctions, and the potential. The next rise 7th May 2024. **7 is a quiet interesting number !**

Chapter 6: May 7, 2024 – The Day of Reckoning:

A Tuesday the world will remember

The Swearing-In Ceremony and Its Immediate Aftermath

May 7, 2024, dawned with a sense of foreboding that permeated the capitals of the world. In Russia, the swearing-in ceremony of the newly elected president was set against a backdrop of palpable tension and heightened security. The event, meticulously choreographed to showcase Russia's strength and unity, was watched by the world with a mix of anticipation and apprehension. As the new president took the oath of office, the air was thick with the unspoken acknowledgment that this day could very well mark a turning point in history.

In the immediate aftermath of the ceremony, there was a brief, almost surreal, calm. Statements of goodwill poured in from various world leaders, each carefully worded to balance the customary congratulations with an underlying message of caution against escalating tensions. However, beneath the veneer of diplomatic pleasantries, the gears of military and strategic planning continued to turn.

Initial Military Movements and Strategic Deployments

Even as the new president's inaugural address echoed with promises of peace and stability, the reality on the ground told a different story. Initial military movements, observed and reported in real-time by a vigilant global media, indicated a rapid escalation. NATO forces, previously positioned in strategic locations in Eastern Europe, were now mobilized to a higher state of readiness. The deployment of additional troops to the borders of Norway and Finland, ostensibly for exercises, was seen by many as a direct countermeasure to the Russian military's own movements along its western and northern frontiers.

In Ukraine, the situation was even more volatile. The proposed British expeditionary force, a topic of much contention, began its preliminary operations under the guise of military training exercises. Meanwhile, Russia, interpreting these movements as provocations, initiated a series of maneuvers that brought its forces to the very edges of the NATO-aligned territories.

The Global Reaction: Diplomacy and Defense on High Alert

The global reaction to the events of May 7 and the unfolding military deployments of May 8 was a mixture of alarm and urgency. International bodies, including the United Nations, called for restraint and dialogue, even as they convened emergency sessions to address the rapidly deteriorating situation. Diplomatic channels, previously avenues for negotiation and peacekeeping, were now flooded with demands and accusations, each side blaming the other for the spiraling crisis.

Social media platforms and news outlets buzzed with real-time updates, analysis, and a torrent of propaganda from all sides, shaping public opinion and further entrenching divisions. The world's citizens, from the cafes of Paris to the streets of Tokyo, watched in real-time as the specter of conflict loomed ever larger. Gaia is on fire.

Defense systems across Europe and beyond were placed on high alert, with missile defense systems in key locations being tested and readied for potential use. Naval forces in the North Atlantic and the Mediterranean adjusted their patrols, while air forces increased their surveillance sorties, all in preparation for a conflict that seemed increasingly inevitable.

As the sun set on ***Wednesday May 8, 2024,*** the world braced itself for what might come next. The events of these two days had set in motion a wave of actions and reactions that could no longer be easily contained. Fake Diplomacy appeared to falter in the face of mounting military preparations, and the hope for a peaceful resolution seemed to dim with each passing hour. The days of reckoning on ***May 7 and May 8*** had not only marked the beginning of a new presidency in Russia but had also edged the world closer to a conflict of unforeseen proportions.

Chapter 7: Beyond May 7 – The Road to War

Escalation and Potential Pathways to Conflict

In the weeks following May 7, 2024, the world witnessed a rapid and dangerous escalation of military activities and rhetoric, lead by UK. The initial posturing and strategic deployments that characterized the days immediately after the Russian presidential inauguration evolved into a series of provocations and counter-provocations. Each action seemed to beget an equally aggressive response, creating a cycle of escalation that spiraled towards open conflict.

The tension was palpable across multiple fronts. In Eastern Europe, NATO's increased military readiness and the buildup of Russian forces along its borders led to frequent skirmishes and incidents. These confrontations, though initially limited in scope, served to harden attitudes on both sides, eroding the last vestiges of trust and diplomatic goodwill.

In the Baltic Sea and the Arctic, the strategic importance of these regions brought an added dimension to the conflict. Naval engagements and aerial intercepts became more common, as both NATO and Russia sought to assert their dominance and secure critical sea lanes and airspace.

The Role of China in the Geopolitical Puzzle

As the conflict between NATO and Russia intensified, the role of China in the unfolding global drama became increasingly significant. Initially, China adopted a stance of cautious neutrality, calling for peace and offering to mediate the growing dispute. However, behind the scenes, China was closely monitoring the situation, weighing its options, and considering the implications of the conflict on its own strategic interests, to defend its borders and Taiwan. It's when US bond selling was initiated that China was preparing for war. In July 2023, the head of the *FED* (US central bank) visited China with the following message : *China not to sell off US debt.* But China does not listen... China's foreign reserves have declined by 20% since *December 2023.* China will take Taiwan, and it would most likely do so to divert attention from a domestic debt crisis problem. Debt crisis is everywhere, the wars are the cover-up for every nations from Europe to US including China.

China's involvement added a complex layer to the geopolitical puzzle. With significant economic and military interests at stake, China's potential alignment or opposition could tip the balance of power. The prospect of a two-front conflict (or more) , involving major powers on opposite sides of the globe, raised the stakes to unprecedented levels.

The July Turning Point: From Tension to Total Confrontation

July 2024 marked a turning point in the crisis. The series of skirmishes and standoffs that had characterized the previous months gave way to more direct engagements. An incident in Eastern Europe, still debated in its specifics but undeniably tragic in its outcome, served as the spark that ignited the powder keg. Casualties on both sides provided the impetus for a shift from limited engagement to open hostilities.

The diplomatic efforts that had sought to prevent the escalation of conflict now seemed futile. The channels of communication, once open and active, became conduits for the exchange of ultimatums and threats. The international community, already polarized, found itself drawn into the conflict, with nations being forced to take sides.

August: The Month of Wars

As history has shown, August has often been the harbinger of conflict. In 2024, this historical pattern repeated itself, with the full onset of hostilities beginning in earnest. The symbolic weight of the month, resonant with the anniversaries of both World Wars, was not lost on the world. This time, however, the conflict was not limited to the European theater but had the potential to draw in global powers across multiple continents.

September 3 and 4: China Enters the Dance pushed by US ?

The involvement of China in early September marked a new phase in the conflict. Initially hesitant to become directly involved, China's decision to provide "defensive support" to Russia was a game-changer. This move, articulated as a response to the "unjust aggression" of NATO, signaled China's willingness to assert its position on the global stage and defend its strategic interests.

The entry of China into the conflict on September 3 and 4 was not just a military maneuver but a statement of geopolitical intent. It underscored the multipolar nature of the world order and the complexity of alliances that could shape the course of global events. The involvement of China not only expanded the scope of the conflict but also raised the possibility of a wider war, one that could involve multiple theaters of operation and a range of military and economic tools.

As July turned into August, and then September, the road to war that had begun in the aftermath of May 7, 2024, had led the world into a conflict of uncertain dimensions and unpredictable outcomes. The turning point from tension to confrontation had been crossed, and the world braced itself for the consequences.

Chapter 8: Avoiding Apocalypse or Not ?

As the conflict escalated across multiple fronts, a narrative emerged that starkly contrasted with the official positions of governments and military alliances. This narrative suggested that, for some, war was not just a policy tool but a necessity. In this context, NATO's aggressive posture and the US's strategic interests were seen not just as responses to perceived threats but as elements of a broader desire to maintain global dominance and stimulate its military-industrial complex.

The Paradox of Peace and War

While political and military leaders spoke of security and defense, a growing chorus of voices from civil society began to question the true motives behind the march toward war. It became increasingly clear that, despite the rhetoric, there was little genuine appetite for peace among the world's power brokers. The stark reality was that war, with its devastating human and material costs, was seen by some as a means to achieve strategic objectives, consolidate power, and sustain the economic interests of the military-industrial complex.

NATO's insistence on military solutions and the US's unwavering support for such approaches were critiqued as evidence of a deeper malaise—a world order that prioritized conflict over diplomacy, and power over peace. The people, those who bore the brunt of war's horrors, yearned for peace, but their voices were drowned out by the clamor of tanks and the rhetoric of their leaders.

Switzerland's Lost Neutrality

Even Switzerland, long celebrated for its neutrality, found itself
ensnared in the geopolitical machinations created by EU. The erosion
of Swiss neutrality was a symbol of the broader degradation of
international norms and principles. Switzerland's perceived shift,
whether through economic pressures, political coercion, or the
strategic interests of its government to follow EC, underscored the
extent to which the conflict had permeated the global consciousness,
leaving few, if any, truly neutral spaces.

The UN's Hopeful Stand : Be the New World Order

Amidst the chaos, the United Nations emerged as a beacon of hope
for many, clinging to the belief that it could serve as the architect of a
new world order once the conflict had subsided. However, the reality
was that the UN's capacity to influence the course of events was
severely limited. International laws were flouted with impunity,
treaties were disregarded, and the UN's calls for peace and dialogue
often fell on deaf ears. The organization's hope to emerge as the
governing authority in the conflict's aftermath seemed increasingly
detached from the grim realities of international politics.

A World of Chaos

The seizure of Russian assets, in defiance of international
conventions, was emblematic of a world order that had become
unmoored from the principles of sovereignty and the rule of law. This
act, far from being an isolated incident, was indicative of a broader
disregard for the norms that had governed international relations. In
the shadow of conflict, the massive debts of governments were
obscured, with war serving as a smokescreen for economic instability
and fiscal recklessness.

The unfolding conflict was not just a battle for territory or power but a manifestation of a deeper crisis—a world grappling with the limits of its post-World War II order, challenged by emerging powers, and driven by the imperatives of survival in the face of existential threats. The pursuit of war by those in power, seemingly in defiance of the widespread desire for peace, revealed the stark divide between the governed and their governors.

As the world navigated this treacherous landscape, the quest for peace became not just a diplomatic challenge but a moral imperative. The voices calling for an end to hostilities grew louder, demanding a reevaluation of the principles that had led humanity to the brink of disaster. The hope for a resolution lay not in the continuation of conflict but in the collective realization that peace was the only path to a sustainable future for all.

Chapter 9: The Future Beyond 2024 :

Worst before to become better

As the global conflict escalated through 2024 and into 2025, the world teetered on the brink of a new era marked by warfare, geopolitical shifts, and internal strife. The ramifications of these tumultuous years would unfold in a series of dramatic and often tragic events, reshaping the international landscape in profound ways.

Maximum War: 2025-2026

By 2025, the conflict that had begun as a series of regional skirmishes had expanded into what could only be described as maximum war. Nations across the globe were drawn into the fray, either through alliances, ideological affinities, or the sheer force of geopolitical pressure. The scale of military engagements grew, with battles raging across multiple continents, in the air, on the ground, and at sea.

The toll on civilian populations was catastrophic. Cities lay in ruins, and the global economy teetered on the verge of collapse. Supply chains were shattered, leading to widespread shortages of basic goods and a humanitarian crisis of unprecedented scale. The world had not seen such widespread devastation since the Second World War, and the international community struggled to respond effectively.

The Rise of Civil Wars: 2025-2029

Amid the international chaos, several nations experienced the eruption of civil wars, most notably in the United States and France. In the US, deep political divisions, exacerbated by the global conflict and economic hardship, sparked violent confrontations between various factions. Martial laws will be imposed. France, too, saw its social fabric torn apart by internal conflicts, fueled by ideological rifts and the pressures of the ongoing global crisis led by EU on-going-regulations.

These civil wars were characterized by their brutality and the profound impact they had on the national psyche. For example, the number of people pouring over the Southern Border each year now exceeds US birthday counts. In the US a country like Switzerland is entering the US... Of course, in both countries, the very notion of unity and shared identity was challenged, leading to a period of introspection and transformation. Muslims are leaving France also.

The End of the USA as we know it: 2029

The conflict and internal strife that ravaged the United States throughout the late 2020s culminated in a dramatic restructuring of the nation. By 2029, the USA, as it had been known, ceased to exist in its previous form. The combination of civil war, economic collapse, and the failure to maintain its global hegemony led to the fragmentation of the country into smaller, more manageable entities, Texas and Florida emerge as new nations.

This disintegration marked the end of an era. The United States' role as the world's preeminent superpower was relinquished, leaving a vacuum that would reshape global politics in the years to come in the profits for China.

The Awakening of China: 2032

Why should China have any reserves in Western bonds and in USD ?

Into this vacuum stepped China, emerging in 2032 as the world's leading superpower. The path to this ascendancy was neither simple nor uncontested. China faced its own set of challenges, get rid of USD and bonds for example, both internal and external, but its strategic patience and long-term planning allowed it to navigate the tumultuous post-conflict world effectively.

China's rise was marked by its emphasis on stability, economic development, and a cautious but assertive foreign policy. By leveraging its economic might, technological advancements, and the strategic foresight of its leaders, China positioned itself as the central player in a new world order.

When you no longer trust someone, you do not do business with them.

Looking to the Future :

A new humanity … AFTER

the Biggest Bond Crash in human history :

10 trillions in Maturity this year only

The transition into the 2030s and beyond was a period of profound change. The legacy of the global conflict and the subsequent rise of new powers forced a reevaluation of the principles that had governed international relations for decades. The world had to confront the reality of a multipolar landscape, where cooperation and competition coexisted in a delicate balance.

The era of maximum war had left deep scars, but it also offered lessons. The importance of diplomacy, the value of sustainable development, and the necessity of global cooperation became the guiding principles for a world weary of conflict and eager for a stable, peaceful future.

As the new superpower, China's role was pivotal. Its leadership in addressing climate change, spearheading economic reform, and promoting global stability was watched closely by the international community. The world that emerged from the ashes of the 2020s was one of cautious optimism, where the potential for peace and prosperity coexisted with the memory of past turmoil.

The future beyond 2024 was uncertain, but it was clear that the events of these years would be remembered as a turning point, a moment when the old world order was challenged, and a new, more complex landscape emerged, because of a hidden debt crisis reformatted in wars.

This is how ALL governments that borrow fail.

We are following the same path worldwide (Europe, US, China).

It is not a question of IF there will be a Sovereign Debt Crisis -

 it is only a question of timing -

Time is Everything

WHEN ?

7th May 2024

The answer.

Christophe Paroni